THE BOOK OF THE
GOAT

THE BOOK OF THE

GOAT

words by Jack Denton Scott

photographs by Ozzie Sweet

G. P. PUTNAM'S SONS   NEW YORK

Text copyright © 1979 by Jack Denton Scott
Photographs copyright © 1979 by Ozzie Sweet
All rights reserved. Published simultaneously in
Canada by Longman Canada Limited, Toronto.
Printed in the United States of America.
Book design by Kathleen Westray
Library of Congress Cataloging in Publication Data
Scott, Jack Denton
The book of the goat.
Summary: Discusses the history of goats,
their habits, characteristics and usefulness,
and six important and popular breeds.
1. Goats—Juvenile literature. [1. Goats]
I. Sweet, Ozzie. II. Title.
SF383.35.S36 1979 363.3 9 79-14321
ISBN 0-399-20681-7

ACKNOWLEDGMENTS

OUR thanks for the help, cooperation, knowledge, and permission to roam their farms so generously given by Helen Hunt and her manager, George Wheeler, of the noted Toggenburg Shagbark Farm, Washington, Connecticut; to George and Vivian Proctor, of Cadillac Farms, Leakey, Texas, famed for their worldwide export of fine purebred goats; and to the Whittenburg Angora Goat Ranch, Rock Springs, Texas, perhaps the nation's largest goat ranch.

We appreciate beyond words their introducing us to one of the most unique animals we have ever met.

OZZIE SWEET
JACK DENTON SCOTT

IF asked who is man's oldest animal friend, most of us would probably answer without hesitation, "The dog."

But there is a good chance that we would be wrong. The goat may well be our oldest animal friend. Since the dawn of history, long before even the most primitive form of writing existed, the goat has been in the company of man, playing an important role in his survival.

Yet for most of us the goat rarely comes to mind. Although we have between four and five million goats in the United States, many of us are unaware that this fascinating and valuable animal exists in such numbers here.

Unfortunately, most of our ideas about goats are mistaken ones, gathered from cartoons of "billy" goats butting people or standing high on trash heaps nibbling away at tin cans. And we've all heard unfortunate expressions such as calling someone on "old goat" or "getting someone's goat."

Who hasn't seen an unkempt goat standing forlornly in a scrubby yard or field tied to a tree and dismissed it as a smelly, unattractive animal?

Actually the goat is among the most intelligent and helpful of our animals. One has only to look at the goats shown here to begin to realize that a revision of its reputation is past due.

What exactly is a goat?

We know the dog, the cow, and the sheep much better than we know the goat. The dog is a favorite pet and companion. The cow gives us milk, cream, and cheese; the steer is a source of beef. Sheep supply us with wool for clothing, and lamb and mutton for food.

What does the goat do for modern man? Why is this animal, one so rich in history, so much more respected in the past than the dog, the cow, or the sheep, not so well known to us? Where does it come from and why do we think that it may be our oldest animal friend?

The answers are fascinating.

The goat, technically, is any of five species of mammals, hollow-horned ruminants (cud chewers), making up the genus Capra of the cow or Bovidae family. The domestic goat, Capra hircus, is the most widely geographically distributed domestic animal. It is found nearly everywhere except in the arctic regions.

The ancestors of the so-called common goat, wild goats, existed over seven million years ago. Among them are the bezoar goat of Iran; the ibex, found in the Alps, the Himalayas, and the Pyrenees; the tur of the Caucasus mountains; and the markhor of India and Afghanistan.

It is believed that the domestic goat is descended from the wild goat of southwestern Asia, and has inherited agility, hardiness, and intelligence from those ancestors.

One fact is certain: the goat has been with us a long time.

One historian records: "Wherever men dwelt in the ancient days, even long before the Age of Pottery, there were herds of domesticated goats. In Africa (even today in some areas), and, in fact, in most places then, man's wealth was computed by the number of goats he possessed." In Africa for many years this social situation was called the "goat standard."

8

Despite the combined knowledge of archaeologists (who study materials from past civilizations), osteologists (who study ancient bones), and historians, controversy exists regarding which is the oldest of our friends, the goat or the dog. Archaeologists do, however, make the flat statement that based on evidence gathered it is obvious that the goat was definitely the first ruminant to be domesticated. They claim that goats, like dogs, were our close associates in the making of historical civilization.

Bones of goats that some osteologists date as far back as 10,000 B.C. were found in the Middle East, at al-Khaim in the Wadi Kharaitun, which runs from Bethlehem to the Dead Sea.

Osteologists have also determined that the goat was the most popular and plentiful of the early domesticated animals. Eighty percent of all animal bones excavated in the early Neolithic settlements of 7000 B.C. such as Jarmo in the Middle East, were of domesticated goats. This same discovery was made in the earliest agricultural settlements of Thessaly, Greece. Eighty-three percent of all bones unearthed were of domesticated goats. There was no evidence of dogs.

Other archaeologists claim that the oldest authentic sign of animal husbandry was found in the lower strata of the city of Jericho, and also near Ur on the Euphrates, the area in the Middle East known as "the cradle of man." Here, the bones of goats—goats that closely resembled present-day domestic animals—were estimated to be seven thousand years old.

It has been established that even before they practiced agriculture, the ancient Egyptians kept herds of goats in the Fayum area. Later, they herded goats over Nile-dampened fields to trample seeds into the soil so the birds couldn't steal them.

Historians have stated that among the early farming people of 6500 B.C., agriculture was secondary to goat-herding, especially in the Iranian villages of Ali Kosh and Tepe Guran. From evidence discovered at Tepe Guran, in Luristan, it is believed that the first occupants of wooden huts anywhere were goat herdsmen.

Known even today as "the poor man's cow," the hardy and resourceful goat then as now could flourish on high, rocky, scrubby land where cattle and sheep would perish.

History tells us that by the third millennium B.C., the Sumerians considered goats so valuable that they could be exchanged for silver or copper. This was before the days of coined gold.

The goat has survived in the Bible, where it is mentioned 136 times. The word "kid" is used fifty-one times, and there are 11 direct references made to goat's milk, hair, and skin. The Old Testament points up their worth, mentioning that Jacob received spotted goats as wages.

It was also the Scriptures that gave us a word we use even today—"scapegoat," or fall guy, one who is blamed for another's wrongdoing.

In the ancient Hebrew ritual, the people gathered on the Day of Atonement while the chief priest confessed over a live goat the sins of the Children of Israel, putting them on the head of the scapegoat, then driving it off into the wilderness. "And the goat shall bear upon him all their iniquities to a land not inhabited…"

Besides using the goat in their rituals, the Hebrews (and all early peoples, even those of the Stone Age) found the goat valuable in practical ways. Goat's flesh

(especially kid) was prized as food, as was its milk. Its hair was woven into cloth, its hide tanned for leather. Tents were constructed of goatskin. The first water bottle and wineskin were fashioned from that skin, as were musical instruments, the harp and drum tops. Goat horns became trumpets.

The dog, as its supporters claim, may have been domesticated as early, or earlier, than the goat, but its uses could not have been as varied, nor could it have been as important an ally.

13

With its strong features and air of dignity, the historic goat was the first animal to appear in ancient Greek and Roman mythology. It was a face to stir the imagination. The god of the shepherds, Pan, son of Mercury, was half goat. The great Jupiter, when an infant, was suckled by a goat. The chariot of the great northern deity Thor, who is commemorated in our Thursday (Thor's Day) was drawn by a pair of goats. Among the ancient Egyptians, one of the most respected gods was the goat Mendes. The Pharaoh Cephrenes thought so highly of goats that he had 2,234 entombed with him near the pyramid of El-Gezeh.

Goat profiles and faces, with and without horns, were engraved on coins, painted on pottery, sculptured on cathedrals, and used as the personal symbol of ancient rulers. Twelve-thousand-year-old paintings of goats have been found on the walls of caves in Europe.

The goat may also have been the first creature to have its name written in the heavens. Capricornus, the goat, has for centuries been the tenth sign of the zodiac. Capricorn is a major constellation in the southern skies and the Tropic of Capricorn marks the maximum southern deviation of the sun during the year.

Yet, with all of this celestial respect, even reverence, for the goat in the past, in the present (except among breeders and those who have made it their business to observe this intriguing animal firsthand) the goat is misunderstood and unappreciated by too many of us.

But if we are to remember the goat from books or legend, why not forget the slander and think of the goat that was Robinson Crusoe's friend and salvation on his deserted island, or Heidi's grandfather in the classic Swiss tale, who although for the most part soured on mankind, found comfort in his goats?

That is what many owners claim to get from their goats—comfort, together with entertainment, sustenance, and even companionship. For the goat is many things to many people, and in some ways is a creature far superior to the other "farm" animals such as the cow, sheep, pig, and even the horse, which are valuable and helpful, but whose personalities are dwarfed beside that of the goat.

Today about four hundred million goats supply sixty percent of the world's population with milk. In the Canary Islands, Spain, and Greece, goats are still driven from house to house and milked at the doorstep, giving much fresher and more nutritious milk than we receive in our tasteless, oversterilized cow's milk in its waxed container at the supermarket. There are about one million milk goats in the United States.

In India, the Middle East, and Africa, in southern Europe and in most of the underdeveloped countries, the goat is the main supplier of milk, cheese, and meat. The meat of the kid is claimed by some to be superior to lamb. Goat hide, which is soft, elastic, durable, and resistant to moisture, is used for gloves, jackets, shoes, and boots. Fine Moroccan leather is made only from goatskin. One of the world's strongest fibers, mohair, comes from the goat.

Although there are over two hundred breeds and varieties of domestic goats, a mere six have emerged as the most important and popular. Five of them are milk or dairy goats, and one is raised for its valuable silky fleece.

Many experts believe that the Swiss have done the most to make the modern milk goat the superb animal that it is. One expert, M. H. French, believes that the ability of the Swiss goats to cover long distances in the Alps has given them strength, good health, and remarkable foraging powers.

So it isn't surprising that of the five best milk breeds, three that came from Switzerland are popular throughout the Western World.

THE SAANEN

THE Saanen is probably the most widely distributed of the dairy breeds. Originating in the Saanen Valley of Switzerland and the cantons of the Bernese Oberland, this Alpine breed is so well liked in its homeland and so widely distributed there that 107 Swiss Saanen associations exist. Some countries such as the United States, where in 1904 ten were imported by F. S. Peer, retain the name; others change it. In England it is called the British Saanen, in Germany the White German Edel goat.

Does stand thirty inches at the withers and weigh a minimum of 135 pounds; bucks stand thirty-five inches and weigh on the average 185 pounds. The face is straight or slightly concave, or "dished."

Breeders consider pure white the ideal color, but light cream or ivory is acceptable. Permissible are spots on the skin and on the upright ears, which point forward. Usually the Saanen is fine-haired, but some strains in Switzerland have long, coarse hair. The breed is usually hornless. It is considered by many to consistently produce the most milk of any breed.

THE NUBIAN

THE attractive, exotic-looking Nubian originated in Nubia in upper Egypt and Ethiopia, and was first imported from England into the United States in 1909, entering through Mexico. They first appeared in Europe in 1860, when the King of Abyssinia sent a young hippopotamus as a gift to Napoleon III. A half dozen Nubian does accompanied the hippo to supply it with fresh milk.

Does stand thirty inches at the withers and weigh on the average 135 pounds; bucks stand thirty-five and weigh 175 pounds and up. Generally hornless, the Nubian has no fixed or preferred color. It can be black, or tan and red, with or without white. Occasionally a Nubian may appear spotted or piebald. The British claim to have improved the breed by crossing it with their own goats. Their Anglo-Nubian is a superior milker.

Most distinctive, with fine, short, glossy hair, the Nubian has unique features, is somewhat long-legged, has an aquiline "Roman" nose, and large, floppy ears which often hang below the jaw. Many consider the Nubians, especially the kids, the most appealing of all goats. They are gentle and affectionate, and at present are probably the most popular breed.

THE ALPINE

THE Alpine, possibly the oldest breed in Switzerland, originated in the Swiss Alps. It spread to and was improved in the French Alps, where it got its most well-known name, the French Alpine. Much the same breed is also called Italian, Spanish, or Rock Alpine, the last being a "manufactured" American breed crossed with Saanens and Toggenburgs. Most of the famous and expensive goat's milk cheeses of France come from the improved French Alpine. Eighteen does and three bucks were imported into the United States in 1922 by Dr. Charles P. DeLangle.

Acceptable does are thirty inches high at the withers and weigh at least 135 pounds; bucks stand thirty-six inches and weigh on the average 175 pounds. It is the largest and rangiest of the Swiss breeds. Both sexes are usually hornless and preferred that way, but those animals that are horned are attractive, the horns and hoofs being a shiny, showy black.

The color combinations of French Alpines are numerous. They are hand-some, alert animals with sharply defined heads and erect ears of medium length.

THE LA MANCHA

THE La Mancha is the most unique goat in the United States because it is virtually without ears. Relatively new here, it is bred from several other species and was imported from Spain and the Mediterranean area. It has a "straight," appealing face, is slightly larger than the Toggenburg, and is acceptable in any color or combination of colors. The hair is short, fine, and glossy.

The La Mancha's almost nonexistent ears are of two types.

The "Gopher" ear has an absolute maximum of one inch, with little or no cartilage. The end of the ear should be turned up or down. This is the only type of ear permitted for registration of bucks.

The "elf" ear has a maximum length of two inches. Its end must be turned up or down, and cartilage shaping the ear is permitted.

The La Mancha is a rugged goat that can withstand much hardship and still produce a substantial quantity of milk high in butterfat. The La Mancha is for the most part hornless.

THE TOGGENBURG

THE Toggenburg, also of the Alpine race, comes from a valley of that name in the canton of Saint Gall in northeast Switzerland, and from the cantons of Lucerne and Schwyz and the counties of Ober-Toggenburg and Weidenburg. It was first imported into the United States in 1893 by W. A. Shafor, who brought three does and a buck from England.

This graceful, gentle animal was the first recognized breed of dairy goat in the United States. Considered the aristocrat of the milk goats, the Toggenburg is somewhat smaller than the Saanen. Does stand twenty-six inches high at the withers and weigh a minimum of 120 pounds; bucks stand thirty-four inches and weigh on the average 165 pounds.

The preferred coloring for the Toggenburg is light fawn to dark chocolate. Probably the most handsome and friendly of the goats, the ideal Toggenburg has a solid color for the body and a white stripe running down each side of the face, from above each eye to the muzzle. Ears also are white, centered with a dark spot; white appears on the hind legs from the hocks to the hoofs, on the forelegs from the knees down, and on each side of the tail there is a white triangle. The hair is short and fine, lying flat. The head is sharply defined, the facial lines slightly concave, the ears upright, pointing forward. Horns sometimes occur in both sexes.

THE ANGORA

THE Angora, named after an ancient town in Asia Minor, may be the most valuable and unusual goat. There are far more Angoras in the United States than any other type of goat.

The first European record of Angora goats appeared in 1554, when Angier Ghislen de Busbecq, a Flemish diplomat, returned from Constantinople, where he had been Ambassador to the Ottoman Empire. Just before leaving Turkey he bought two Angoras which he presented to Emperor Charles V. The Angora, however, has not been too successful in Europe.

The fleecy little goats were brought to South Africa in 1838 and a major industry, the production of mohair, soon started.

Angoras were brought to the United States in 1849 by James A. Davis of Columbia, South Carolina, who had been sent to Turkey by President Polk at the request of the Sultan, who wanted to experiment in the production of cotton. Subsequently, Davis received nine Angoras as a gift from the Sultan. He presented six of them to Richard Peters of Atlanta, Georgia. In 1925, 117 Angoras were imported from South Africa and sold at public auction in Camp Wood, Texas. From that year on, the raising of Angoras became an important industry in Texas.

Usually much smaller than the dairy or milk breeds, Angoras have been crossbred in the United States to increase their size. Our Angora does stand twenty-six inches high at the withers and weighs seventy five to 120 pounds; bucks are thirty inches in height and weigh at least 175 pounds.

Both sexes have wide, spiraling horns, the buck's longer and thicker, sometimes attaining a length of two feet. A hornless strain has also been developed. The hair on the face, lower legs, and ears is white, soft, and silky. Except for the face and lower legs the body is covered with a thick, fine, white, lustrous fleece which hangs in locks or ringlets, reaching a length of from eight to ten inches, nearly touching the ground. One Angora, amazingly, grew fleece forty-one and a half inches long that weighed over twenty-two pounds. Tails are short, the ears long and pendulous.

Although their meat—"mutton" or "chevon"—is sold and prized by some, Angora goats are raised principally for the production of mohair. Unlike the other goats in this book, the Angora doe does not usually produce twins, nor does she bear a kid at the expense of her own body weight. If feeding conditions are poor, and the Angora doe loses weight, she aborts.

REPORTS of the goat's intelligence go back to Pliny, the ancient Roman philosopher, teacher, and author, who wrote, on the authority of an eyewitness, Mutianus, the following:

"Two goats coming from opposite directions met on a very narrow bridge, which would not admit either of them of turning round, and in consequence of its great length, they could not safely go backwards, there being no sure footing on account of the narrowness, while at the same time an impetuous torrent was rushing rapidly beneath. Accordingly, one of the goats lay down flat, and the other walked over it."

Some historians claim that Pliny sometimes used this anecdote to pose a question to his students: Which of the two goats was more intelligent? Answer: The one that waited for the other to lie down.

History also records that in the medieval animal shows goats were the most popular, and considered even more intelligent than dogs. Goats could quickly be taught to perform balancing tricks, climb almost impossible-to-negotiate inclines, operate a seesaw, and nimbly run on high suspended planks.

Not only has the goat proven its intelligence, it is also among the cleanest of animals, a much more selective feeder than cows, sheep, pigs, chickens, and even dogs. Goats will eat nothing that has been contaminated or that has been on the floor or the ground, except growing plants and other vegetation. They are so fastidious that they won't eat hay thrown on the floor of their sheds or barns, so most goats are fed from a manger above their heads.

Smelly? Cleanly kept does and their young are as odorless and as particular in their habits as a pedigreed pampered house cat. During the breeding, or rutting, season, bucks have an odor that emanates from two glands behind the horns that may be objectionable to us, but not to other goats.

With some animals different breeds are not easy to distinguish among the young. Not so with the goat. Kids are obviously Toggenburgs, Saanens, Nubians, or Alpines almost from the moment of birth.

Brimful of personality, radiant representatives of their breeds, goat kids instantly captivate with their wide-eyed innocence, their naive friendliness, and their precocious alertness.

But character is also an adult goat copyright. It is evident in the proud, high-held head, the direct, questioning gaze, and the alert, friendly demeanor, which is not the tail-wagging, subservient manner of the dog. Goats look you in the eye, know and recognize you as a friend, and respond like no other farm creature.

They come when called, follow their owners, and show affection to humans whom they like. These are always humans who return that affection.

The noted poet and famous biographer of Abraham Lincoln, Carl Sandburg, whose wife bred goats, said, "Goats are friendly. You can talk with them. A cow doesn't know what you are saying. But these goats come up very quietly and brush against you, as if to say, 'Isn't life good?'"

Kids respond to kindness and have long memories, especially when it comes to something to eat. Kitchen handouts are remembered, and that famous goat-kid personality is put into play to accelerate the opening of a door and the appearance of a hand with favorite food.

Goats are not the frenzied, dashing, perpetual motion creatures they have often been characterized as being. If they are happy in their surroundings, goats are relaxed and in control. They take siestas. They respond to human friends when asked to change pastures; they follow the person they know and respect. Roundups and noisy chasings are unnecessary in well-managed goat herds. The exception is the Angora herd, which must be assembled for shearing.

For many years goats were used in Tibet to carry salt across the Himalayas. They were more valuable than pack horses or mules because they didn't have to be led. They followed the people whom they knew. Also, in negotiating the difficult mountain terrain, they were much more agile than other pack animals. And, because of their intelligence, it took less than thirty minutes to "break" a goat to carry a pack.

This cooperation of goats with humans stands out in the history of the animal. In the United States, from about 1870 to 1910, harness goats pulling children and adults in all kinds of carts and wagons were as popular as ponies and there were more than twenty thousand goats trained to harness.

Most goat owners claim that not only are goats more pet than farm animal, but their affection can be turned on and off, even to the point of giving milk for the people they like and withholding it from those they dislike.

Versatile, producing more milk on less food than a cow, a goat can produce that milk in high mountains, deserts, and even the subtropics—regions where cattle cannot even range. The goat also provides us with the greatest quantity of high-protein food in relation to its own body weight of any domestic animal. The normal purebred milk goat, weighing little more than one hundred pounds, averages about a gallon of milk a day. Some top milkers give as much as eight quarts a day. One goat produced an astounding 5,750 pounds (over 2,500 quarts) of milk during her 305-day official test, and that record may even have been bettered.

Goat's milk carries its own homogenizer. The evenly distributed fat globules are so small that the law of gravity does not effect them as it does cow's milk, in which cream rises to the top unless it is mechanically homogenized. This perfect emulsion in goat milk and the soft curd make it more easily digested. Goats also change carotene in milk into a maximum amount of vitamin A. These factors make it a perfect food for infants who require special feeding (goat's milk has saved thousands of their lives) and those who cannot tolerate cow's milk. Most goat breeders who sell milk have testimonials from people who claim to have been cured of arthritis, heart disease, eczema, asthma, hay fever, stomach ulcers, and other digestive disturbances after a diet of goat's milk.

Goat breeders, however, do not ascribe magical qualities to goat's milk. Claiming that it is neither a medicine nor a cure-all, they say that the milk is a good-tasting, nutritious food ideally suited for everyone and especially helpful to individuals with allergies and poor digestion.

It is a fact, however, that India's famous leader, Mahatma Gandhi, lived mainly on goat's milk for over thirty years, and it is also claimed that his great vigor and stamina came largely from that diet of goat's milk, cheese, and butter.

England's Winston Churchill, another of the world's great leaders, also a man of hardiness and endurance, was an enthusiastic devotee of goat's milk.

Goat's milk cheese is the gourmet's delight and includes French roquefort, Norwegian gjetost, Greek feta, and the Trappist monks' Chevret, which they have made famous. These are not the only cheeses made from goat's milk, but are among the best known.

Although it is not a milk goat, the Angora, because of its fleece, may be the most valuable goat in the dollars and cents category—and also the most mysterious. Historians do not agree, but many believe that the Angora originally came from the mountains of Tibet. Ancient tribes brought the small hairy goats with them from the Himalayas into Persia, then Asia Minor. Turkey eventually became the country best known for Angoras.

Texas has the most Angoras in the United States today. They are ranged in large herds, or flocks like sheep, and in most ways are cared for like sheep. They are rounded up for change of pasture and for shearing with highly trained "Angora dogs."

More intelligent than sheep, the Angoras do not need the nipping and the hard, consistent herding by the dogs, but alertly take their direction.

The word mohair, the name for the fleece that is sheared from the Angora goat, comes from an Arabic phrase "chosen as the best." Also called the "diamond fiber" (because of its value, about four dollars a pound), it is used in the manufacture of quality yarns, suits, wigs, knitwear, sweaters, hats, dress fabrics, upholstery, and wall and floor coverings.

In an average year, mainly in Texas, the United States produces about twenty million pounds of mohair from one and a quarter million Angoras. The only other countries that produce it in any quantity are South Africa and Turkey.

The Angora averages one inch of mohair a month—about twelve pounds yearly. However, in especially well-fed and well-managed herds, the annual yield can be as much as twenty-two pounds per animal.

In most areas Angoras are sheared twice a year, spring and fall. In the colder regions they are sheared only in the spring, with some ranches "caping"—leaving a four-inch strip of fleece down the back to afford some protection from the weather.

A skillful shearer, using power clippers, can shear an Angora clean in two minutes.

Angora bucks (and those of some other breeds) are trained to act as "Judas" goats. With the male goat's leadership qualities and dominant traits, it is easily schooled to lead a flock of sheep in any direction—to be sheared or to the slaughterhouse. Hence the name Judas.

Although some people call female goats "nannies" and males "billies," this is considered a little precious by those who know the animals best—the breeders. The correct word is doe for the female and buck for the male, the same terminology used for deer. Young bucks of a year of age are called bucklings. Does are doelings. If a doe has only one offspring, it is referred to as a singleton. The Old Testament term kid, for either male or female under one year, still applies.

The male of the goat species—with horns, like the shaggy Angora, or without, like the Alpine, Saanen, Toggenburg, or Nubian—is not easily mistaken for anything but a male. With his long beard, he exudes dignity and power, and has an air of command. Physically, as with most animal species, he is larger, blockier, often with a coarser coat than the female.

Even with beards, which are common in females, the bearded goat-ladies are unmistakable. They are definitely feminine, slimmer of limb, usually with finer hair. Some, like the Toggenburg does, are deerlike in their coloring and in their graceful movements, and the milk-white Saanen does are the perfect picture of feminine elegance.

Thus, although it is not likely that goat sexes can be confused, they can be mistaken at a distance, for both doe and buck can have horns. The horns of the buck, however, are larger and longer.

It is possible that the current practice of breeding hornless bucks to hornless does has kept most of the domestic goat race in a ratio in which less than half now have horns. The kids that are born with horns or shortly thereafter develop the buds of horns are debudded. This is done three days or so after birth, painlessly, with a hot iron.

Bucks with horns aren't downgraded by breeders, but it is easier for them to handle a buck without horns and less likely to cause complications. Bucks in rut are aggressive. Their horns are dangerous to other bucks, to does who aren't ready to breed, and even to the owners of the goats.

The reason, however, that professional breeders do not try to raise completely hornless goats is genetic. If a breed is hornless for too long a period, the bucks may become hermaphrodites: that is, animals with characteristics of both sexes. Bucks of this type could be useless as breeders, their masculinity impaired.

But usually, unless the herd numbers in the hundreds, one buck—horned or otherwise—is sufficient for breeding purposes. During the breeding season he can be isolated and the receptive females introduced to him. So horned males, given good management, should not cause problems.

Masculinity in normal males not only is never in question, but is positively awesome. There is the case of a buck that escaped from his pen and bred an entire herd of forty-five does before he was caught in slightly more than an hour. As each breeding usually takes very little time, this probably wasn't any kind of a record.

The breeding runs from August through January, often peaking in November. At the end of the 150-day gestation period, one to four young (twins being normal) are born, on the average an equal number of males and females.

Professional breeders prefer to mate does at eighteen months, but it can be accomplished earlier if the doe is vigorous and well-developed. The lifespan of domestic goats averages about twelve years.

Life for the newborn normally begins with the obvious pregnant bulge of the mother, then the actual birth, which involves much straining by the doe while she stands. Usually the birth is rapid. First, a bag of transparent membrane appears, encasing the muzzle of the kid. Then the head appears.

The doe rests briefly now. Then, as she strains, the membrane-bag bursts and the kid is delivered. It slips out and tumbles to the ground unhurt, a tangle of wet legs.

If there is to be a second birth or more, which is usual, it happens in a few minutes. Goats seldom have trouble "kidding," and often give birth to their twins in a field without assistance or anyone knowing about it.

Now, with the wet kids on the ground before her, the doe cleans off the sticky mucus that covers them. This is a time-consuming job, but she keeps at it until they are dry.

One of the amazing assets of kids is that they can stand and walk after they are dried off by their mother, sometimes in mere minutes. Unlike puppies, rabbits, and some other animals, kids are born with eyes open, with tiny teeth, and with muscles so coordinated that they can move about almost immediately.

Soon after they are dried off, the kids are hungry. Finding the teats that will give them the warm, life-sustaining mother's milk is a task they must complete by themselves. The mother can't help much here. It's a search-and-find endeavor, with some clumsy misses before the teat connection is made.

If goats are being raised for milk, the kids are taken from their mother in a matter of days, sometimes even hours, after they are born. This is done not only to continue to obtain salable milk, but for other reasons. Kids can become rough with their mothers as they grow hour by hour and their hunger increases accordingly. Breeders also claim that the majority of these kids become rather wild during this period and remain so. They mean wild, in the sense that the kids have not learned that people control their feeding and their management.

Also, goat mothers are affectionate, and the sooner their kids are taken from them the less traumatic the separation. Kids that have remained with their mother for approximately a three-week period before weaning become so attached to her that they do not want to leave her. They also try to continue nursing for as long as the doe will let them.

Less experienced goat owners allow the kids to remain with the parent until they are weaned by her, leaving it up to her to do the disciplining if the kids get too rough in their feeding or try to overextend the nursing period. There are few sights in nature more appealing than a female goat with young, taking them along as she grazes, nuzzling them affectionately, playing the supervisory role of parent as only she can.

There is, however, a way to attain both goals, the commercial and the natural, in the raising of milk goats. Some breeders are adopting the technique, first used in Israel, of leaving the kids with their mother during the day, then separating them at night. That way the kids still receive the beneficial mother's milk, and the breeders keep the milk that is produced during the night.

Feeding kids taken from the parent can involve a simple milk bottle and hand-feeding or a mechanical contrivance with many rubber teats. Whatever the method, the intelligent kids quickly learn where the milk comes from and how to start it flowing.

With it their lifeblood also starts flowing and their bouncing and frolicking begins. For them the world becomes one big playpen. In about three weeks they will require less milk, begin imitating the adults in eating grass, and soon will be weaned. Occasional feedings of milk may continue until the kids have grown sufficiently and prefer natural fodder.

A leaping, gamboling kid is a joyous sight. Some of the jumps are incredible, almost vertical. The kid seems to make them on impulse. Standing peacefully, suddenly it soars into the air in a feeling-good-to-be-alive bound. That leap has become part of our language. "Caper," which is the short form of the French *capriole* (taken from the Italian *capriola,* or leap of a goat) means jump, dance, or caper about. It can also mean a wild escapade.

If there is one subject all goat owners agree upon, it is companionship. Goats do not like to be alone. They prefer to be with their own kind, and if kept alone their spirits and appetites lag. They become lonely and irritable. If they can't have a goat companion, they will settle for a human being. But the fact is that goats like goats.

Goats are gregarious. Visual contact between individuals is maintained within the herd. To keep this contact between particular goats that like and associate with one another, there are frequent liftings of heads while grazing to see that all is secure and nothing unusual is happening.

Goats are quiet, calm, and confident when part of the herd, but they can quickly become nervous, even panic-stricken, if separated from it.

Since goats have personalities, there are differences in their makeup. Some are aggressive, some submissive, some curious, some placid. Put together, this melding of personalities form what is called a herd hierarchy, not unusual in the animal world.

The most aggressive and dominant buck becomes the leader of the herd, and the strongest doe heads the female group. Newcomers to the herd quickly discover into what niche of the society they belong and establish their own rights.

The dominance of the leader is so strong that if the herd follows him to the main grazing area, they will all browse along the way according to the pattern established by the leader. If he stops to crop grass, so do they. If he moves, they follow.

Does permit their kids to wander farther from them than sheep do. This could be because kids are more intelligent than lambs. When they sense danger, or anything abnormal, kids crouch close to the ground and remain as motionless as wild creatures do under the circumstances.

One scientist studied a herd of fourteen goats, concentrating on the dominance system. To determine if the aggression of members of the herd, or the pattern of dominance, would be altered if the goats were frustrated, feed was withheld from them for varying periods. Nothing changed appreciably. The herd's social structure was so soundly formed that the aggressive goats remained in control; other members of the herd who had attained their own status also retained it. There was more fighting among the most aggressive goats than usual, caused by the frustration of not finding food. Other than that the situation remained socially normal.

Goats are so skillful and have such a catholic taste while grazing that as few as six can easily browse, or "brush off," an acre of heavy growth, changing it into pastureland for cattle and sheep, animals that don't have the goat's proficiency.

With the toughest mouth of any ruminant, a goat can consume, without harm and with benefit, such "inedibles" as nettles, thistles, briars, and brambles, converting this waste vegetation into milk and meat. (It is this tough mouth that has led to the myth that goats will eat anything, even tin cans.) In relation to its size, the goat can eat twice as much daily as a sheep or a cow. According to goat expert David McKenzie, "one third of its total body capacity is available to accommodate food in the process of digestion."

In Sweden the versatility of the goat's feeding habits was put under the microscope of science. Tested goats ate 449 out of 574 varieties of plants. The goat herd could live just about anywhere and at any height, except in areas of heavy ice and snow, thriving in infertile regions on a diet that would have destroyed cows and sheep. Goats, summed up the scientists, are geared for survival.

But in the end (or is it the beginning?) the life-style of the goat herd revolves around the propagation of the species—around the birth, care, and training of the young.

One of these bouncing, captivating kids will grow from a gangly buckling into a lusty full-grown buck, the new leader of the herd.

It will become the prototype of the animal that became a deity in ancient times.

This he-goat will walk in the dignity that is still *tays,* the Arab expression for the goat and for nobility of bearing. In its conduct as leader it will exemplify why the Hebrews named it *atude,* the word for prince, and why the ancient Assyrians respected such a goat so much that they erected monuments in its honor.